FINNEY COUNTY PUBLIC LIBRARY
605 E. Walnut
Garden City, KS 67846

Jason's First Day

Written by
Valerie Busic

Illustrated by
Jeff Meyers

Copyright 2004 by the
Osteogenesis Imperferfecta Foundation
ISBN 0-9642189-4-1   8.50

Donation of this book was made possible
through a generous grant from the

Stirling Foundation

This book is donated in memory of

Richard Devereaux

Jason was awake even before his mom came to tell him it was time to get up. He got out of bed, then put on his leg braces and new school clothes.

"Well, good morning Jason!" his mom said, smiling. "You look very handsome in your new school clothes!" She combed Jason's hair, adjusted his braces and straightened his shirt, then asked, "Are you hungry?"

"Not really. Can we just leave now?" Jason asked. "I mean, would it be bad to get there a little early?"

"I'll make you a deal," Jason's mom said with a smile. "You eat a little bit of your cereal, I'll finish getting ready, and then we'll get going."

"I'll try," Jason said.

A little later his mom asked, "Are you ready, kiddo?"

"Sure, let's go!" Jason answered. A few minutes later, mom stopped the van in front of the school. Jason stared through the window. It seemed bigger than he remembered it.

"Good morning Jason!" Miss Mary said as she slid the van door open. She was going to be Jason's helper in school. "Are you ready for your first day?"

"I think so," Jason said, trying to smile.

"You are going to have a great time," Miss Mary said.

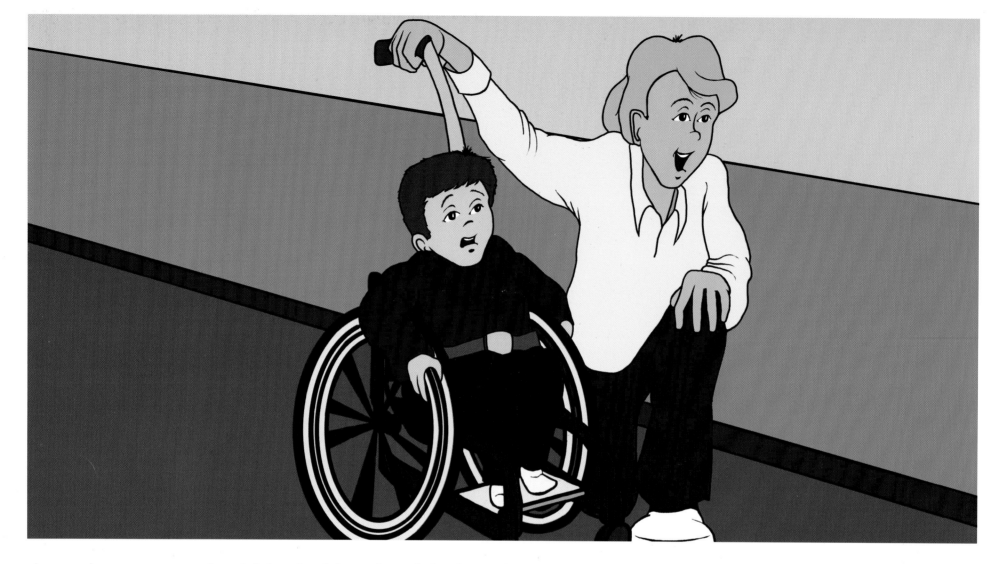

Jason's mom pushed him in his wheelchair to his new classroom, while Miss Mary followed close behind with his walker. "There must be a million kids here today," Jason said as they carefully went through the hallways.

When they got to room 115, Miss Mary knelt down and pointed inside. "Here we are, Jason. Are you ready?"

Jason peeked inside. Many children had already arrived. Some laughed and talked while others sat quietly and looked around the classroom.

Jason took a deep breath, and wheeled into the room. His cheeks grew warm as everyone seemed to stop and look at him. Jason gave them the best smile he could and waved. The other kids smiled and then went on with what they were doing.

"Hello, Jason," said his teacher, Mrs. Williams. "Come on in and make yourself comfortable. Your seat is over here."

Jason's mom showed Mrs. Williams how to help Jason out of his wheelchair and into the chair by his table. Then Miss Mary set his walker next to the table while his mom moved his wheelchair out of the way, but close enough for Jason to use later.

"Hey, my backpack is the same as yours!"

Jason looked to see a boy sitting down in the seat next to his. "I'm Ben. Hey! We even have the same shoes on!" Jason looked down at his feet and both boys laughed.

"Good morning, class." Everyone began to settle down as the teacher spoke.

"Welcome to kindergarten! My name is Mrs. Williams, and I will be your teacher this year."

Mrs. Williams walked around the room slowly and said the name of each child in the class. She said she wanted to make sure she said each name correctly. She came to Jason last.

She winked at him and then said, "Class, I would like you all to meet Jason."

"Some of you may have noticed that he arrived here this morning in a wheelchair."

"Jason has osteogenesis imperfecta, or OI. This means that his bones can 'fracture,' or break *very* easily. We will all have to be extra careful not to push or bump into Jason."

Mrs. Williams picked up a piece of chalk and held it up for the class to see. "What will happen when I drop this large piece of chalk on my desk?"

"It will break," Ben announced. Sure enough, when it dropped, it broke into three pieces.

"You are right, Ben. Chalk breaks easily. Jason's bones are very much like this piece of chalk. Jason will be using a wheelchair and a walker to help him move around safely. The braces that he wears on his legs help protect them and make them stronger."

"Miss Mary will also be here to help Jason throughout the day." Miss Mary waved to everyone and said hello.

"It is very important for all of you to understand that you can't 'catch' OI from Jason. It's not like having a cold. It's just part of how he is made. I'm sure you'll soon find that Jason loves to do many of the same things that you do."

13

Mrs. Williams smiled at Jason. "Does anyone have any questions?" she asked. One boy raised his hand. "Will he break his bones in this class?"

"That's a very good question, Anthony!" Mrs. Williams said. "It is possible that Jason might break a bone while he is here with us at school. If Jason does get hurt, we will make sure that he is taken care of right away."

Marissa, the girl sitting right in front of Jason, asked "Do your legs hurt right now?"

Jason shrugged his shoulders and said, "Actually, they feel pretty good right now." Some of the kids smiled when Jason said that.

Mrs. Williams said, "All right children, if you have any other questions, please ask me, or Miss Mary, or Jason."

Jason learned all sorts of new things. He practiced writing his name. He even learned that he and Ben, the boy who sat next to him, liked to play the very same video game. In no time at all, the morning was gone. Mrs. Williams told everyone that they would need to start getting ready to go to lunch.

With Miss Mary's help, Jason got back into his wheelchair and headed to the lunchroom a few minutes early. This way the hallways weren't as crowded and there was less chance of someone bumping into him.

In the lunchroom, Jason couldn't wait to open his new lunch box to see what his mom packed for him. Ben sat next to Jason, so they decided to open their lunch boxes together. They both had their favorite, cheese sandwiches with no crust!

When lunch was over, it was time for recess.

Jason looked around at all the kids. "May I color on the sidewalk with Ben?" Jason asked Miss Mary.

"Of course," she said. Miss Mary helped Jason sit on the ground next to Ben and together the boys made some very colorful pictures as they talked.

"Can you run and play catch?" Ben asked.

"I'm not supposed to run," Jason said. "But I like to play catch. Right now, though, my legs are healing from fractures." Jason pulled up his pant leg to show Ben his braces. "See? These help hold my bones straight so that when they are better, I can do all sorts of stuff. I play lots of video games and read books when I can't do other things."

19

After recess, the children went back to class for story time. Some of the children sat on little carpet squares, while others sat in special reading-time chairs.

Near the end of the day, it was time for art. Mrs. Williams told the children they could paint pictures of whatever they wanted. When they were done, Mrs. Williams asked each child to talk about their paintings.

Anthony painted a big green and pink fish. Marissa painted a big blue swimming pool.

When it was Jason's turn, he held up his painting and said, "I drew you, Mrs. Williams!"

Mrs. Williams smiled. "That is lovely, Jason."

"My turn! My turn!" Ben shouted, jumping up from his chair. "This is a picture of my new best friend, Jason." Ben turned to Jason and added, "Here, I want you to have it."

Jason smiled and took the painting. "Thanks, Ben."

Just then the bell rang. It was time to go home. Jason said goodbye to Ben as Miss Mary helped him gather his things.

When they got outside, Jason's mom was there to greet them. 'Hey, how was your first day?" On the way to the van, Jason showed his mom all the things he worked on through the day.

"Mom, I made a new friend today. His name is Ben and he made me this picture. It's a picture of me!"

"That is a wonderful picture," his mother said as she hugged Jason and gave him a kiss on the forehead. "Let's go home, and you can tell me more about your day while we have a snack."

Jason turned and waved good-bye to Miss Mary. "I promise I'll see you in the morning," he said.

The End

A message for teachers:

During the early school years there is an emphasis on similarities and differences- between living and non-living things, between plants and animals, and between people and people! It is the perfect time in a child's education to create awareness of people with Osteogenesis Imperfecta (OI) and other disabilities. We are all people yet everyone is different.

Acceptance of differences among people comes from understanding. Understanding is the ultimate goal of obtained knowledge. As educators, we have a responsibility to teach our children that first and foremost, people are people. Any differences help to make us individuals and all individuals are treated with respect.

This guide has a dual purpose. It is for the classroom teacher's use as a reference and resource to help integrate an awareness of OI and other disabilities into the curriculum for young children. It is also meant to provide the teacher with information that may ease the transition of the child with a disability into the classroom.

We hope this guide will assist in your lesson planning so that disability awareness can be woven into all parts of your curriculum. The more children learn and understand, the greater the acceptance will be that people are simply people.

Osteogenesis Imperfecta: An Overview for Educators

Osteogenesis imperfecta (OI) is a genetic bone disorder characterized by low bone mass and bone fragility causing bones to fracture easily. For example, falling, tripping, sitting down on a hard surface, even coughing can cause a fracture. There are six described types of OI (I-VI) that vary in degree of severity and clinical presentation from mild to severe.

Jason, the child in the story, has OI type IV which is clinically considered a moderate form. School-aged children with OI have a wide range of abilities, limitations and needs.

Children with mild forms may walk independently, have no visible signs of the disorder, and may only fracture occasionally. Children with moderate forms may demonstrate a wide range of abilities and may use a wheelchair, walker and/or crutches. Leg braces may be worn for support when standing and walking. Children with severe forms of OI may also require a power wheelchair and occasionally supplemental oxygen. They may be very small for their age.

Children's physical abilities vary and may be altered temporarily due to a recent fracture or surgical procedure.

Ideally, it is advisable to discuss the child's functional abilities in detail with his parents or caregivers prior to the child's first day of school.

Children with OI, all types, usually have normal to above-average intelligence, and typically participate in a regular curriculum. Instructional and physical environment modifications may be required for safety and to promote independence. Some children with OI benefit from assistive technology devices for energy conservation such as lightweight writing instruments, pencil grips and adaptive scissors.

Teach all staff that children with OI are capable of functioning at grade level, their small physical stature is not to be mistaken for immaturity, and these children must be treated the same as their peers. They should be held accountable all school rules and standards of behavior.

Federal education laws, Individuals with Disabilities Education Act (IDEA) and Section 504 of the Rehabilitation Act of 1973, ensure appropriate test access and modifications for individuals with disabilities. Accommodations for classroom instruction and/or test modifications may include an extra set of books for home, additional time to travel between classrooms, preferential seating, a special chair and/or desk arrangement. These accommodations may be included in a written plan either with an Individual Education Plan (IEP) or a "504 Plan."

Contact your state education department for established accommodations. Further suggestions can be obtained through the Osteogenesis Imperfecta Foundation (see Resources).

Seek Advice from Parents or Caregivers

Encourage meeting in advance with the child, his parents, and all staff who will work with the child to familiarize yourself and the staff with the child's individual needs. Understanding the child's abilities will ensure the child's independence in school and minimize the child's and teacher's initial fears or apprehensions. Discuss privacy and agree on what will be said about the child's disability in front of peers. Some parents may volunteer to talk to your class about OI. Discuss the best way classroom staff should communicate with parents (e.g. a notebook or teleconference). Everyone who interacts with the child should be knowledgeable about handling day-to-day activities and emergencies.

You may want to inquire into the following areas to allow for a smooth transition into the school:

Fractures

Children with OI may break a bone due to an obvious trauma, such as a fall, or through normal activity such as coughing or bumping into a table while in school. Establish a written policy with the parents in regard to handling the child and the use of his equipment. Establish a written fracture/emergency plan and keep an emergency contact list in an established place for substitute teachers, school nurses and or alternate staff personnel (see sample on page 34). Detailed information in an established location allows for good communication between the school and the family and informs alternative school personnel when the teacher is unavailable. It is important to remember that no one should be blamed when a fracture occurs.

Assistive Devices

Children with OI may utilize an assistive device to move and may require assistance for daily living skills. Discuss the child's physical abilities and inquire about all devices used: walker, crutches, wheelchair, and braces. Discuss and have parents demonstrate how to safely lift and transfer the child, and how to assist with coat and clothing if necessary.

Physical Activity

Children with OI may fatigue easily when performing physical activities. Discuss the child's physical endurance level with the family. Does he require frequent rests when walking or propelling his wheelchair? Providing a second set of books to keep at home relieves the child with OI from having to carry heavy books to and from school or to and from classrooms. Minimizing trips to and from a locker or cubby, perhaps through the use of a backpack, can also prevent fatigue.

School Environment

Even a building that is built to accommodate children with disabilities may be hazardous to children with OI, since any trip or bump can result in a broken bone. Walking through the child's planned routes to the playground, auditorium or restroom can help to identify areas that will be difficult for crutches, walkers or a wheelchair. Items on high shelves may be out of reach, heavy doors or high thresholds may be serious obstacles. Elevators may be necessary to move up and down between levels. Automatic openers may be necessary on heavy entry doors.

Personal Aide

Children with OI may attend school with a personal aide or a paraprofessional. Discuss the role the aide should play to ensure the child's maximum participation in classroom instruction, physical independence and peer socialization. To encourage self-advocacy, staff should be reminded to talk directly to the child, not through the aide. If a personal aide is not assigned to the child, a buddy may be selected to assist the child with access to materials in the classroom, lunchroom and during special activities.

Adaptive Seating

Children with OI may require adaptive seating, including a foot rest, to provide postural support and keep the child at eye-level with peers during tabletop activities. In general, children with OI have good fine motor skills. However, they present with weakness in their arms and hands causing them to fatigue with activities requiring repetitive motions such as cutting. Discuss the child's typical endurance levels when performing tabletop activities, so frequent rest periods can be built into activities if necessary. Adaptive equipment and alternative lightweight writing instruments may be helpful. Beanbag chairs, cube chairs or a "boppy" pillow can be useful in providing protection while allowing the child to be close to others during floor activities. The OI Foundation can be consulted for information regarding assistive technology and classroom accommodations.

Wheelchair Use

Children with OI who use wheelchairs will need designated time during the day to stand or lie down out of the wheelchair. This promotes optimal body alignment and prevents muscle contraction. Parents, teachers, nurses and a physical therapist (if available) may jointly decide on the best arrangement.

Toileting

Children with OI may require assistance for toilet transfers or may require a bathroom area large enough to accommodate a walker or wheelchair. Determine a bathroom plan and discuss if the child will utilize the class bathroom, an alternate bathroom or whether his toileting needs will be addressed with the school nurse.

Fire Evacuation

Establish a fire evacuation plan with parents and administration. Determine the safest way to transport the child and the wheelchair safely from the area. This should be clearly posted for all school staff to follow.

Transportation

The child may require special arrangements for busing either for transportation to school, during field trips or other school excursions. If there is a written plan for the child, whether it be an IEP or a 504 Plan, make sure all details are included on the document to ensure continuity if the transportation company changes.

Home Study

Children with OI may require home study periods following a fracture or surgery. Teachers can help the child with OI stay connected to the classroom during these periods by exchanging classroom and home journals either daily or weekly, sending classroom art and craft projects home for the absent child to complete, or requiring the child with OI to present a special report upon return to school.

Seek Advice from Support Services

School therapists may provide direct and indirect therapeutic services to children with OI to increase the child's access and participation in the learning environment. The therapeutic staff may be consulted in regard to the physical management of the child in school. The OI Foundation has numerous resources if the therapists are unavailable or unfamiliar with OI.

Physical Therapy

Children with OI may typically receive physical therapy (PT) or adapted PE services. The physical therapist may assist the child with gross motor delays which may limit mobility in the school environment. They may be consulted about adaptive equipment for seating and mobility concerns in the school environment.

Occupational Therapy

Children with OI may typically receive occupational therapy (OT) services. It may be helpful to consult with the child's OT about physical, sensory and cognitive functioning challenges. Occupational therapists may evaluate children with OI for adaptive equipment and assistive technology devices to enhance their learning experience in the classroom.

Hearing Loss

Some children with OI have hearing loss. Discuss with the parents the use of assistive hearing devices and typical accommodations which might be necessary such as preferential seating and/or the assignment of a buddy to repeat instructions. A speech-language pathologist may be consulted about the use of hearing devices such as an FM trainer or transmitter (a device which amplifies the teacher's voice) and may be helpful in designing a classroom set-up to enhance the child's listening ability.

Safe Recreational Activities

Children with OI can participate in recreational sports and games provided precautions are carefully considered. The parents and child with OI can be asked to provide teachers with a list of activities the child enjoys at home. Creating a list of safe games the child enjoys both indoors and on the playground will be helpful to school staff when working with the class.

Activities can be adapted when necessary if safety or physical restrictions are a concern:

- Basketball: Replace the basketball with lightweight balls such as foam or inflatable balls. The basket can be lowered if arm reach is a concern.

- Baseball or t-ball: Replace the ball with a wiffel ball and use a plastic bat.

- Tennis: Use lightweight or badminton racquet with lightweight or inflatable ball.

- Hockey: Tie a plastic floor hockey stick to the wheelchair and replace the puck with a larger lightweight ball.

- Consider non-contact physical games like "Red Light, Green Light, 1-2-3" rather than tag games.

- Use an elevated sandbox to allow wheelchair access with lightweight sand tools.

- Bring tabletop activities to the recess area such as trading cards, checkers, bubbles, action figures or drawing.

- Think about clap games where another child's physical force is not a concern.

Sample Letter to Parents:

Dear Parents:

I would like to share some information about a member of our class who has a bone disorder. This disorder is called osteogenesis imperfecta or OI. It is also known as "brittle bones."

Children with OI have fragile bones that break easily. They also have weak muscles. Because their bones do not grow as much as usual, some children with OI are short for their age. OI is usually not life threatening. Most children with OI go to school and grow up to have careers and families just like their peers.

Children with OI like to do the same things as other children their age. Sometimes they need special equipment to help them get around or keep their bones safe, such as braces, crutches, a walker or a wheelchair. Children with OI like to be treated the same as everyone else. Our classmate will participate in all classroom activities, recess, and even P.E. with close supervision. We are all reminded to be careful, to always be gentle and not push or pull a child or a piece of the child's equipment.

Your child should never be afraid to play with a child who has OI. Children with OI play with their friends at home and visit the homes of their friends. When a fracture occurs, children with OI are usually very capable of instructing an adult in what to do until help arrives. No one should ever be blamed when a child with OI breaks a bone.

If you have any questions about OI or about the classroom program, I will be happy to talk with you.

Sincerely,

Mrs. Williams

33

Sample Emergency Instructions for a Child with OI
(To be given to other caregivers, teachers, etc.)

My child has Osteogenesis Imperfecta, which causes his/her bones to be very fragile and break easily. Extreme care should be taken to prevent (Insert child's name) from being bumped or lifted carelessly. My child has had numerous fractures, and is your best source for determining what to do in case of a fracture.

In case of a fracture, proceed as follows:

1. Do not move him/her if at all possible. S/he will be in pain and need time to calm down. There is no need to rush. Let him/her tell you where the fracture is, and please do not move that limb.

2. If it is necessary to move him/her for safety reasons, do so very carefully and slowly, being careful to support the injured limb and move it as little as possible.

3. Call (parent's name) at (parent's phone number). If you can't reach him/her, call (alternate name and phone number).

4. My child's orthopedist is (insert name). The doctor's phone number is (phone number).

5. Please do not call an ambulance or transport my child to the hospital unless the injury is severe and the people named here cannot be reached.

6. (optional: There is a signed PRN on file in the Nurse's office if my child needs pain medication.)

7. Don't forget to comfort other children or adults who may be upset or feel responsible for the fracture.

8. Sometimes, my child can get bumped, may cry a bit, and then settle down. Quite often, s/he has aches that prove not to be fractures, or are little "cracks" that we do not treat. Please let him/her be the judge and determine whether his/her level of discomfort requires any action.

I hope this has helped. It means a lot to my son/daughter to be included in all activities.

Signed _____ date _____

Resources

To promote disability awareness and self-esteem among your students, incorporate storybooks and media resources which include characters with physical disabilities into your classroom library. Contact the National Information Center for Children and Youth with Disabilities (NICHCY) for an extensive guide to children's literature and disabilities. The following books have been recommended by elementary education teachers who have had experience with children with OI and have used these resources in their classrooms to promote disability awareness and self-esteem:

Storybooks:

Carlson, Nancy L. (1990). *Arnie and the New Kid*. New York: Viking.
-*Arnie needs to use crutches following an accident and begins to understand the limits and possibilities of his classmate who has a wheelchair.*

Curtis, Jamie Lee. (2002). *I'm Gonna Like Me: Letting off a Little Self-Esteem*. New York: Harper Collins
-*A young girl learns to like herself.*

Litchfield, Ada. (1976). *A Button in Her Ear*. Illinois: Albert Whitman & Company.
-*A girl with a hearing deficiency relates how hearing is detected and corrected with a hearing aide.*

Maguire, Arlene. (2000). *Special People, Special Ways*. Texas: Future Horizons, Inc.
-*Conveys the message that although painful at times, being different can be glorious.*

Mayer, Mercer and Gina. (1992). *A Very Special Critter*. New York: Golden Books.
-*A new child critter that uses a wheelchair goes to school.*

Meyers, Cindy. (1999). *Rolling Along with Goldilocks*. Maryland: Woodbine House, Inc
-*Baby bear uses a wheelchair.*

Parr, Todd. (2001). *It's Okay to be Different*. Boston: Little, Brown and Co.
-*Discusses similarities and differences among people.*

Senisi, Ellen B. (2002). *All Kinds of Friends, Even Green!* Maryland: Woodbine House, Inc.
-*A child with a wheelchair befriends a disabled iguana.*

Videos:
(The videos listed below include children with OI.)

Sony Wonder/ Sesame Street (1997). *Elmocize* Children's Television Workshop (1996).
-*Kara is a child with OI type IV. She talks about the importance of exercise and participates in an exercise class.*

The Wiggles. (2002). *Wiggly, Wiggly World*. Hit Entertainment.
-*A child with OI participates in several group singing performances.*

Music:

Petrucciani, Michel. (1999). *Solo Live* (CD). Dreyfus.
-*Jazz pianist and composer with OI Type III has been heralded as one of the best French musicians ever.*

From the OI Foundation:

Plan for Success: an Educator's Guide to Students with OI (video and booklet)
-*A 15-minute video that guides educators and parents through planning steps that will help children with OI to fully participate in all school activities. The video comes with a supplemental booklet for educators and parents that provides detailed information on applicable education laws and requirements, adapted physical education, mobility accommodations, overcoming architectural barriers, what to do when a fracture occurs at school, and how educators can help a child's peers understand OI.*

Osteogenesis Imperfecta: A Guide for Medical Professionals, Individuals, and Families (booklet)
-*Basic information about the types of OI, inheritance, diagnosis, and treatment.*

Growing Up with OI: A Guide for Families and Caregivers (book)
-*Addresses the most common questions parents, family members, and caregivers have about raising a child with OI. The book includes a chapter on educational issues.*

Growing Up with OI: A Guide for Children (book)
-*Written especially for elementary school-age children, this book focuses on the same issues as the adult version. It encourages children to focus on their strengths and abilities, and provides problem-solving advice for challenges they may face.*

Osteogenesis Imperfecta: A Guide for Nurses (booklet)
-*Intended for nursing professionals and nursing students, or as a resource for those unfamiliar with OI. This is a comprehensive guide to assist nursing professionals as they work with patients with OI. Offers practical insight into diagnosis, family education, standard treatments, medical procedures and care for patients of all ages.*

Osteogenesis Imperfecta Foundation
804 W. Diamond Ave., Suite 210
Gaithersburg, MD 20878
(800) 981-2663 or (301) 947-0083
fax: (301) 947-0456
bonelink@oif.org
www.oif.org

Linking "Jason's First Day" and Disability Awareness to the Early Education Curriculum

Science: Human body lesson: similarities/differences between bones with and without OI. Children with OI typically have curved long bones placing them at additional risk of fracture. May include bone shapes; compare bones that are curved versus bones that are straight. Compare properties of materials which are dense with properties which are fragile. Create fragile bone (soak a chicken bone in bleach to make it brittle) and compare with normal bone. Demonstrate how much easier it is to break it. The child with OI could share his experiences with fractures, show his x-rays and talk about casts and bone healing.

Health: Keeping teeth and bodies strong. Discuss nutrition, exercise and dental care. The child's physical therapist and or the school nurse could be a guest speaker to describe ways "Jason" may exercise to become stronger. Some children with OI also have Dentinogenesis Imperfecta which affects dentin, the substance under the tooth enamel, causing the teeth to look gray and fracture easily. This could be included when discussing the color and shape of children's teeth. When discussing a unit on body image, point out that a wheelchair is considered part of a person's body and should not be pushed without permission.

Social Studies: When discussing a unit on People in the Community include people in wheelchairs, people with OI, people who have had fractures, people with braces. When working on a unit about citizenship, include safe play, rule following, and inclusion. Invite the children to participate in thinking about how to make the classroom more accessible for the child with OI and how to include him/her in activities (lunch, recess and field trips). Don't allow the child with OI to ignore school rules. He must be accountable for his actions as all other children are.

Structured Play: When considering multisensory play experiences, make it a point to include appropriate tactile and kinesthetic activities for the child with OI. Consider materials such as clay, model magic, finger painting, sand, rice and water which may encourage gentle hand strengthening while working on fine motor coordination. Safe kinesthetic experiences may include parachute play, dancing, puppetry, or lightweight balls. To promote mobility, set up activity stations so movement, whether in a wheelchair or with a walking device, is encouraged.

Discussion Guide

The following questions are provided as suggestions for using *Jason's First Day* as a springboard for age-appropriate discussions about physical differences, inclusion, and osteogenesis imperfecta. The goal is to help young students become comfortable with mobility aids and at ease with a classmate who has a physical disability. It has been our experience that given the opportunity, young students will raise many questions of their own, expecially about wheelchairs, and will show concern for the health of their classmate.

Pages 1 & 2

Background:
A child with OI will have the same concerns and sense of excitement as any other child who is starting school or entering a new environment. Because OI causes some difference in physical appearance, the child may have additional concerns.

Questions:
Who wore something special for the first day of school?
Who woke up early on the first day of school?
Why do you think Jason wanted to get to school early?

Page 3

Background:
Proper nutrition is very important for all children. It helps them be ready to learn and it helps them stay healthy. A healthy diet with enough calcium, vitamin D and other nutrients is essential for building strong bones.

Questions:
How many of you ate breakfast today?
Did you know breakfast is the most important meal of the day?
Do you think Jason will eat more for breakfast tomorrow?

Page 4

Background:
Visiting the school before the first day of class is important and very helpful to the child with OI, parents, caregivers and teachers. They will have a chance to meet each other and tour the building and playground and solve any accessibility problems ahead of time.

Questions:
Who visited the school before opening day?
Who has older brothers or sisters here at school?
Was it a good idea for Jason to visit the school before the first day?
What do you think he did during the visit?

Discussion Guide

Pages 5 & 6

Background:

A child with OI may have an aide or helper during the school day. Children with OI may also show different levels of walking ability depending on the situation and their degree of severity.

Questions:

Miss Mary is Jason's helper. Let's name some other helpers here at the school.

Do you think the hallways in our school are crowded?

What happens when a lot of people are in the halls?

Why do you think Jason has a wheelchair *and* a walker with him at school?

Pages 7 & 8

Background:

Children are naturally curious. A child's wheelchair, walker, crutches or leg braces will attract attention. In this story, Jason's teacher sets the tone for friendliness and minimizes awkwardness. It can help to have samples of your student's mobility equipment available for the rest of the class to touch and explore. This provides them an opportunity to ask questions, and also provides an opportunity to explain that the student's equipment is like any body part, and should not be touched without permission.

Discussion Guide

Page 9

Background:
Except for their fragile bones, children with OI are just like other children. They are interested in the same things, and have the same needs for learning and making freinds.

Questions:
Questions should be posed to help identify all the things the children have in common.

Pages 10 - 13

Background:
The children in the class will feel more comfortable if OI is explained to them in simple terms as soon as possible.

Questions:
Let's think of some more examples of things that are brittle- that break easily.

How do we take care of things in our homes that break easily?

Has anyone else here ever had a broken bone?

What does a doctor do to help bones heal? (sling, cast)

Page 14

Background:
Since it is possible that a child with OI may fracture a bone while in school, it is important to reassure the class that adults at school are ready for any emergency.

Questions:
Let's name some of the people at school who will help if anyone gets hurt.

What can we do to keep each other from getting hurt?

If one of our classmates gets hurt, what should you do?

Page 15

Background:
Determine ahead of time whether you, a parent/caregiver or the student will answer questions about his/her OI.

Discussion Guide

Page 16

Background:

Children with OI show the full range of intellectual abilities as their peers. They should be expected to participate fully in the education program. When moving to different rooms within the school, it is often safer to allow the child with OI to leave a few minutes early to avoid crowded hallways.

Questions:

There are a lot of things for us to learn in school. Let's make a list of some of the things we'll learn.

Why do you think Jason left early for lunch?

Pages 17 - 19

Background:

Children with OI have the same interests as their peers and the same need for socialization experiences. It is a good idea for the parent/caregiver and school staff who supervise children during recess to meet prior to the start of the school year to set appropriate guidelines for their particular student.

Questions:

What are some of our favorite things to eat for lunch?

What are some of our favorite games to play inside? Outside?

How do we show someone we want to be friends?

Did you know there are sports designed for people with wheelchairs?

Discussion Guide

Pages 20 - 22

Background:
See pages 29-30 for suggestions about setting up the classroom so the child with OI can move around safely. The goal is to have the child with OI be at eye level with his/her peers for all activities within the classroom. As everyone becomes familiar with each other, the novelty of a child using a wheelchair, walker or crutches will wear off. Children can become very accepting about a classmate who has a physical difference.

Potential Questions:
Can you find Jason's wheelchair in these pictures?

How can you be a good listener during story time?

Does the wheelchair make any difference when Jason is painting a picture or listening to a story?

Pages 23 & 24

Background:
Making friends and establishing routines help all children become more secure at school. It is particularly important to the child with a physical disability like OI.

Questions:
Do you think Jason had a good day at school?

What do you think he liked about school?

Let's imagine what will happen at school tomorrow.

This book was made possible by a generous grant from

The Braitmayer Foundation

We wish to thank the Bright Start Story Book advisory council.

The council included parents, teachers and children with OI.
This book would not have been possible without their inspiration and advice.

Gayle and Katrina Bache
Olney, MD

Sherry Frost
Bellefonte, PA

Michelle and Nicole Hofhine
Camarillo, CA

Dan and Jeffrey Krudys
Leawood, KS

Brian Kuhn
Silver Spring, MD

Maureen McCabe, P.T.
Albertson, NY

Theresa and Jonathan Reed
Worthington, OH

Barbie and Beth Simmonds
Arlington, VA

Special thanks to:

Willam Bradner, Mary Beth Huber, Marie Maffey, Eleanor Alice Neal
The Henry Viscardi School , Albertson, NY
The YMCA Ayrlawn Program Center, Bethesda, MD

Notes: